**WISE**
CHOICES

GW00703209

# HAPPILY EVER AFTER?

### Coping with the pains of divorce

MARTIN HOLDT

*Warmest.*
*Greetings.*

*Martin Holdt*
*mph @ global. co. za.*

*'Get wisdom, get understanding;*
*do not forget my words or swerve from them.*
*Do not forsake wisdom, and she will protect you;*
*love her, and she will watch over you.*
*Wisdom is supreme; therefore get wisdom.*
*Though it cost all you have, get understanding.'*

**Proverbs 4:5–7**

DayOne

© Day One Publications 2007   First printed 2007

Unless otherwise indicated, all Bible quotations are from The Holy Bible, English Standard Version®

Copyright © 2001 by Crossway Bibles, a division of Good News Publishers

All rights reserved.

A CIP record is held at The British Library        ISBN 978-1-84625-096-5

Published by Day One Publications  Ryelands Road, Leominster, HR6 8NZ

☎ 01568 613 740  FAX 01568 611 473  email—sales@dayone.co.uk  www.dayone.co.uk

☎ In North America call 888-329-6630

No part of this publication may be reproduced, or stored in a retrieval system, or transmitted, in any form or by any means,
mechanical, electronic, photocopying, recording or otherwise, without the prior permission of Day One Publications

Editor: Sue Holmes

Design and Art Direction: Bradley Goodwin  Illustrations: Susan LeVan and Bradley Goodwin   Printed by Gutenberg Press, Malta

To my wife, Elsabe, and my beloved children to whom I owe
a debt which I can never repay

# Commendations

*Divorce has become one of the tragedies of our times and needs to be faced with realism and honesty. In this superb book Martin Holdt has done precisely that, writing with a pastor's heart and an unflinching adherence to biblical principles. Here is a straightforward resource crammed with clear, practical and spiritual counsel. I know of nothing better.'*

**John Blanchard, Author, Apologist and Evangelist**

*Most booklets on divorce are theological treatises on the Scriptural grounds for divorce and remarriage. This book is refreshingly different, for it is a pastoral and practical appeal to married couples to resolve the problems leading to divorce for the sake of God and the children, as well as advice on how to cope with separation, should it occur. Thoroughly biblical and lovingly written, it will under God be a valuable tool for pastors to give to all who are thinking of or struggling with divorce.*

**Brian A Russell, Virginia, USA, Author and retired Baptist pastor, having served churches in South Africa, Zimbabwe and the USA**

*Divorce is one of the one or two most painful things we human beings can go through. For your spouse to tell you that having lived with you and gotten to know you they now do not want to live with you and know you intimately any longer must be one of life's deepest hurts. To enter into the bond of marriage with 'stars in your eyes' only to have it become 'sand in your eyes' brings deep misery, guilt, depression, self-pity, recrimination, bitterness, loneliness and isolation. Having said that, the life of divorced people is made worse because there is much bad counsel given to hurting divorced people.*

*That is why Martin Holdt's book is such a gem. Despite its small size, it packs a wallop of wholesome, healing medicine to those who will drink deeply from it. Martin is a sensitive guide to hurting, sin-sick people. He is this because he is* primarily a Bible man—one who knows the God of the Bible and his Son, Jesus Christ, and the life-giving, healing remedies God has for his people. While not condemning, Martin is not sugar-coating the problems and neither does he ignore bad medicines. Rather Martin gives old but untried, true but ignored counsel from God's Word which is balm for the soul.

In a phrase, try it, you will like it, and it will heal your soul.

**Steve Martin, Pastor, Heritage Church, Fayetteville, GA, Trustee of the INSTITUTE OF REFORMED BAPTIST STUDIES at Westminster Seminary, California**

… trenchantly biblical, fervently compassionate, thoroughly sensible. Pastor Holdt so deftly combines realism and hope in this treatment of divorce.

**Dale Ralph Davis, former Professor of Old Testament, Reformed Theological Seminary, Jackson, MS, Minister at Woodland Presbyterian Church, Hattiesburg, Mississippi**

# CONTENTS

# All about divorce

Getting divorced is a daily occurrence in our society. You, my reader, may not be divorced but if you are not careful, it may become a possibility. Even if you have never experienced divorce, there is always someone either in the family circle or the community who needs understanding because he or she has suffered the pain of divorce.

In my childhood, divorce was rare in the community where I lived. In the seven years we lived in a particular town, the break up of a marriage would be the talking point of the entire region. In those days, a definite restraining factor was the children. Today things are different. Unfortunately, certain misguided sociologists suggested in the 1960s that children were not as adversely affected by divorce as was thought before. How eager people were to believe such a false idea! The divorce rate sky-rocketed.

There are many reasons for divorce but the most important one is the absence of a fear of God. The Bible tells us that the natural man has no fear of God: 'Transgression speaks to the wicked deep in his heart; there is no fear of God before his eyes' (Psalm 36:1). When Joseph was tempted to have an illicit affair with another man's wife, this was the powerful restraint which kept him from breaking up a marriage. As he put it, 'How then can I do this great wickedness and sin against God?' (Genesis 39:9). When people carelessly first entertain the thought and then actually set the stage for the dissolution of a marriage, it is always because of the absence of a fear of the God who says he hates divorce. (See Malachi 2:16.) There are many other factors which tragically make divorce easy. The media does. Soap operas on television often cheapen marriage and people who engage in adulterous affairs are portrayed as heroes. It needs to be remembered that behind all the stories the media churns out, there is a philosophy of life which begins to occupy the minds of people who become absorbed by what they see and read. Biblical values are subtly attacked and made to appear old-fashioned, ridiculous, out of date, not 'with it'. The world responds and it is not long before the lowering of standards increases the incidence of divorce.

Another factor is the increasing number of women in the labour market. This in itself is not wrong, but it is unfortunately true that the high level of social contact between men and women at work has given rise to thousands of broken marriage relationships. People see each other at work at their best, well dressed and well groomed, very competent and slightly mysterious. When they get home after work, there is little to attract the eye to the person who happens to be their life partner and who looks very plain and ordinary, and, may we say, familiar. Comparisons are made. Could a better marriage deal be contracted if the present one were terminated?

> **When they get home after work, there is little to attract the eye to the person who happens to be their life partner and who looks very plain and ordinary, and, may we say, familiar.**

All along the devil misleads. People sink *en masse* into sin and into a disregard for the laws of God. Mid-life crises also have their part to play. This is particularly true of men who are anxious not to be thought of as growing old and unappealing. When a love affair begins with a younger woman, the man reckons he still has what it takes!

Is divorce permissible? It is so important to stress the fact that God never intended a marriage to dissolve. To our first parents he announced: 'Therefore a man shall leave his father and his mother and hold fast to his wife, and they shall become one flesh' (Genesis 2:24). He never meant that unity to be broken by anything except death. Jesus re-emphasized this when he stated that they are no longer two but one: 'What therefore God has joined together, let not man separate' (Matthew 19:6; Mark 10:8). The Bible teaches that not even conversion to the Christian faith is an acceptable reason for divorce. Even then, it is only permissible if the unconverted spouse no longer wishes to have a believing spouse as a marriage partner. (See 1 Corinthians 7:10–16.)

To any reader who may be seriously contemplating severing a marriage bond, I ask you to consider in earnest if this is indeed the only option. Have you considered the necessity and value of Christian counselling? Do you realize how many strained relationships have been resolved by help sought from wise and competent marriage counsellors? Do you truly wish to add to the guilt of an already judged nation?

This last point needs to be stressed, for we often forget that when things go wrong in a country, it is not because of political issues, but always and only because of spiritual and moral decay. In the Scriptures, we read that whenever God's people kept and honoured his laws, all was well with them. But as soon as they disregarded and broke those commandments, everything else fell apart. War, poverty and a host of other problems beset the nation. Do not blame competent and incompetent politicians for the condition of the world. See how we, and others, have transgressed the laws of God. Do we not get what we deserve?

> **To any reader who may be seriously contemplating severing a marriage bond, I ask you to consider in earnest if this is indeed the only option.**

If you are considering the termination of your marriage, you need to ask yourself if you can afford to let your children suffer. They most certainly will. Or, is it a case of the grass being greener on the other side? Think again. Someone once said this: 'Divorce, instead of solving two problems, often creates four.'

Divorce is serious and sad. It grieves the Holy Spirit. It is contrary to God's original plan for man. It breaches two fundamental commandments, namely love for God and love for one's neighbour. Love really is putting the other person's interests first. (See 1 Corinthians 13:4–7 and Romans 14:19.) Marriage is sacred and divorce is displeasing to God. Think twice before seeing your lawyer.

If, perhaps, you have recently been divorced and have not remarried, consider seriously going back to the wife or husband of your youth to experience the glory of reconciliation.

Do you know that an exceptionally high percentage of divorced people cherish the idea of reconciliation? It is not all that difficult. Perhaps it only requires that one puts one's pride in one's pocket and apologizes for the part played in the sad end to the relationship and then is willing to appear hand in hand with one's former spouse before the living God with a fresh pledge to make the marriage work this time. This has happened before and it can happen again. Make your marriage work with the help of God and the assistance of those he has appointed as his servants in this world. For your own sake, your children's sake and for the sake of others before whom you wish to be an example. Glorify God in your marriage vows.

One of the most important means for keeping divorce away from the door is to put one's thought life under the control of the Holy Spirit. 'For as he thinks in his heart, so is he,' the Bible teaches in Proverbs 23:7 (NKJV). If a man or woman therefore continues to entertain thoughts detrimental to the marriage bond, there will be a gradual erosion of confidence in his or her partner. An accumulation of negative thinking about one's situation may one day culminate in a fixed determination to walk out of the marriage. The devil plays havoc with the thought life of many, many people. We do not realize this.

When he spoke to Eve in the Garden of Eden, it was not an audible voice that she heard and she did not see the devil in person. He was disguised. As she stood contemplating the pros and cons of taking the forbidden fruit, she probably reckoned she was debating with herself as to the rights and wrongs of the proposed action. This is exactly what happens to us.

Here is someone who thinks his or her marriage is not up to scratch and starts fantasizing about another one, not realizing the devil is funnelling lies into his or her brain. The Bible teaches us to put to death thoughts of that kind and to think soberly and righteously. (See 1 Peter 1:13.) Think God's thoughts after him regarding marriage. God gives marriage partners to each other and even if things are not quite what they used to be, Jesus, who changed water into wine at a wedding, can turn an ordinary marriage into an extraordinarily happy experience. In spite of one's partner's faults, there are virtues, too, if one cares to look hard enough and there is probably more to be grateful for than to complain about.

Most important of all, think more carefully and prayerfully about God in the matter of marriage. Remember the promises made on your wedding day—to keep yourself for your marriage partner—were made before a watching God. Do not take lightly the fact that he took seriously the promises made. Therefore, an account will have to be given to God for any breach of trust. For the present it may be possible to get away with it, but at the end of the day no one will. On what the Scriptures call the 'Day of the Lord', when nations will be assembled before the Righteous Judge of all the earth to give account of themselves (see Romans 14:12, Hebrews 4:13 and 1 Peter 4:5), there will be those who will shamefacedly have to admit to treating with utter carelessness the sacred ordination of marriage. They will deeply regret that they ever thought it was possible to walk in and out of marriage as one would in and out of a shopping mall. They will wish to live life over again and do a better job of handling God's commandments.

> **They will deeply regret that they ever thought it was possible to walk in and out of marriage as one would in and out of a shopping mall.**

On the other hand, there will be a teeming multitude of couples who will, with deep gratitude, thank God for the grace he gave to keep them faithful to their marriage promises. They will praise him for the help he gave them when they had to work through sticky patches and for the fact that such testings only deepened their relationship in the end. They will thank God for having made marriage a blissful experience for them, as marriage was his idea and he meant it to be great. Into which group will you fall?

# The real reasons for divorce

During a recent conversation with friends, reference was made to couples who had been married for twenty years and more and who were now heading for the divorce court. The inevitable question arose: why does this happen? Having given some consideration to the matter and having realized how sensitive this issue is, especially for those who have been affected in this way, I shall address it once more for the sake of others who may become involved.

Divorce has reached epidemic proportions. If the situation gets worse, and there is no reason to believe it will not, both society and the church will be heading for serious problems. Perhaps, one of the antidotes to divorce is to look into the reasons for its happening. I do not have a long list of causes. In fact, I can narrow it down to three. It is not necessary to accept many of the current reasons given for marital strain. If you are capable of dealing with the following three issues, you will enjoy a lasting and happy marriage.

## 1. Temptation
Temptation is the name of the game. The vast majority of marriages are adversely affected because of a third party entering the scene. Unfair and irrational comparisons are made and infidelity is the result. We have just about forgotten how real temptation is in the human life. When Jesus taught his disciples to pray, he insisted that they should not forget to ask: 'Lead us not into temptation' (Matthew 6:13).

Everybody is tempted daily in one way or another. When a marriage is happy, as God intended it to be, Satan is unhappy and he will make every effort to sow distrust between the wedded pair, to offer an attractive alternative, and then to find ostensibly good reasons for ending the contract and entering into a new relationship. He comes up with suggestions such as incompatibility and proves himself to be what he has always been, the father of lies.

There are no two people on earth who are perfectly compatible as partners, because of our fallen natures, our differing temperaments. Therefore, we have to work at relationships. In the long run, it is simply not true that opting out of one relationship and entering into another provides a better state. Emphatically, it does not. It is not acceptable to God merely to say, 'I made a mistake marrying my first partner,' and using that to end the marriage and to start another.

Remember, Satan tempts! He tempts us where we are most vulnerable. He tempts in order to rob us of happiness. He tempts by presenting alternatives. But his rewards, at the end of it all, are bitterness and misery. He loses no opportunity to tempt people, including Christians, and everywhere people fall for his deceit.

He uses other people to tempt us, as he did in the life of Joseph, when Potiphar's wife became the instrument. Someone at the office or at the club shows another person above average attention, then begins to flatter that person, and before long, defences are down and the person is already half way into the trap. Words smoother than honey flow and terms of endearment are so blinding that it is not possible to see the difference between love and infatuation. Before the person knows what has happened, he or she is in the embrace of a stranger. To justify the diversion from the path of righteousness, abuse and false accusations are heaped on the one who happens to be the rightful marriage partner.

> **Temptation is the name of the game. The vast majority of marriages are adversely affected because of a third party entering the scene.**

If a man acts like this towards his wife, he will cause her to panic. As a result of the shock to her system, she may react violently and, unbeknown to her husband, Satan is right there leading him further along the path of temptation. He begins to feel even greater justification for pursuing an illicit relationship with someone who seems to be so much more gentle, understanding and kind. He is being hoodwinked. While tensions at home increase to the point of affecting the children and their performance in life, he capitalizes on every opportunity to spend more time with the other person, despite the fact that he is incurring the displeasure of a watching God. Perhaps he has not taken cognisance of the

Bible's warning: 'Can a man carry fire next to his chest and his clothes not be burned? Or can one walk on hot coals and his feet not be scorched? So is he who goes in to his neighbour's wife; none who touches her will go unpunished' (Proverbs 6:27–29).

We no longer seem to have the will to fight the devil. It is time to repent and to stand up to his crafty schemes. When you know in your mind something is wrong, never let your heart be carried away by evil desires. The moment you detect a glimmer of temptation, admit it and take it to God.

Believe it or not, but the best thing to do under these circumstances is to pray for the person who is being used as an agent of temptation. Henry Martyn, the famous missionary to India, once felt unusually attracted to a very beautiful girl. He was single and certainly an eligible bachelor, but he felt that his life's calling was to exercise a ministry as an unmarried man. He did something unusual but it was decisive in his battle against the devil. He prayed for the purity of the girl concerned and the mutual attraction died. Satan is an evil spirit and his sales promotion is impurity, which he sells at a special discount. It might look good to all external appearances, but it will lead to disaster.

Jesus showed the devil up for who he really is and he conquered him at the cross. Hide in Christ, and whenever you are tempted, make much of the sympathy and help of a great Friend and God, who was himself tempted as we are, yet without sin. (See Hebrews 4:15.)

### 2. Impatience

This is the second reason for divorce. Things begin to go wrong in the marriage. The lines of communication break down, nothing is done to deal with the difficulty, and matters get worse. Because of the erosion of mutual confidence, the point is reached where impatience masters one or both parties. They look for an escape route and divorce seems to be the easy way out for one or both.

Scripture never leads us to believe that running away from problems is the solution. Thank God, he never saw the world in that light. The mess the human race brought upon itself did not result in a 'hands off' approach on God's part. He tackled the problem head on. He did the best he could do and it cost him the best he could give, his only Son. It meant pain and suffering, worse than the human mind can ever conceive, but it resulted in glory and a marriage relationship between Christ, the Bridegroom, and the church, his bride, which is destined to be to the everlasting honour of a wonderful God.

Similarly, in marriage relationships we need to bear that in mind and apply it to our situation. God gives a man the woman to whom he is married. God gives a woman the man to whom she is first joined in Christian wedlock. Rough passages along the way are not meant to be excuses for an impatient and intolerant capitulation from the impasse. They are meant to enrich both husband and wife as they roll up their sleeves and resolve the issues that have caused conflict, in prayer to the only one who can enable them to do so.

Impatient attitudes in marriage are, after temptation, one of the biggest causes of the breakdown of relationships. Patient dealing with the issues pays enormous dividends and the happiest couples are those who can say, 'We have problems; let us work at them.' Recently, I met a couple who had been married for decades. They indicated that early in their marriage they encountered trauma which might have been justification for a parting of the ways. But they resisted that thought and with patience, fortitude and prayerfulness resolved their troubles. They were happier and much more mature for it.

If you feel the tensions of interpersonal strife in your marriage, be patient while you work through the issues which are a threat to your marital and personal stability.

### 3. Godlessness
Godlessness is undoubtedly the greatest cause of divorce. How can two people be expected to live happily in each other's company if their primary relationship with God is either non-existent or defective? The closer one is to God, the closer one will be to one's spouse. The further one wanders from God, the more estranged one will be from one's marriage partner. The most powerful factor in

Joseph's resistance to Potiphar's wife was his relationship with God. Precisely because he enjoyed deep fellowship with the Lord, he could say to that heathen woman, 'How then can I do this great wickedness and sin against God?' (Genesis 39:9).

Everything Scripture says about man's sinful condition is summed up in the words: 'There is no fear of God before his eyes' (Psalm 36:1). In addition, there is no fear of the dreadful consequences that await those who carelessly tread underfoot God's rules for life. Few people seem to shudder at the Bible's warning that we reap what we sow. While we may get away with it for some time, possibly for a number of years, it catches up with us in the end. Even worse still is the prospect of one day facing God, the Judge, with a track record spoilt by deliberate disobedience to God's command concerning marriage. That is an awful prospect.

To treat marriage lightly and to forget that this was God's first gift to man after creation is to slap a loving and kind Creator in the face. Among the worst crimes on human record is a disregard for God's own personal involvement in the marriage bond, when he says, 'What therefore God has joined together, let not man separate' (Matthew 19:6). That is why godlessness is a primary reason for divorce.

In summary, and more positively, may I ask that you heed my appeal. If you are married, avoid all forms of temptation, work patiently at the problems which inevitably crop up in any marriage situation and, above all, learn to be godly together with your partner—in fact, so godly that you will become more attractive to each other as time goes on, because God himself becomes more endeared to you as the only one who can make your relationship sweet and lasting.

**Everything Scripture says about man's sinful condition is summed up in the words: 'There is no fear of God before his eyes' (Psalm 36:1).**

# Coping with divorce

Divorce happens suddenly and unexpectedly to thousands of people. Jim Smoke *(Growing Through Divorce, Harvest House)* identifies three stages in divorce. The first stage is the shock of it. When this happens, it seems incredible. Surely, not me? This was the furthest thing from your mind. But it has happened. You are about to join the ranks of those who have to tick the word 'divorced' on forms which require one to indicate one's marital status. This causes pain.

Stage two is the stage of adjustment. It is impossible to lament what has happened, so one has to work at a new situation and learn more than ever before to take one day at a time.

Stage three is the stage of growth. Unfortunately, many divorced people miss out on this experience. For any person sensible about such a tragic event, there must be a point where it is possible to start growing again spiritually in the divorced state.

How does one handle divorce? Many emotions strike forcefully in the experience. There is grief; there is anger; there is loneliness. Is it possible to cope? Indeed, it is possible. Bearing the following ten factors in mind will help a person cope:

Firstly, feel closer to God than ever before. Believe it or not, it happened to him! Long ago, God said that he and his people were bonded together in something akin to a marriage relationship. Even in the New Testament the church is said to be married to Christ. However, the day came when God had to say to his people, 'Surely, as a treacherous wife leaves her husband, so have you been treacherous to me, O house of Israel, declares the LORD' (Jeremiah 3:20). What a tragedy! God was grieved about his children's unfaithfulness and the fact that they had broken their relationship with him.

When a believer goes through a divorce, the best place to find comfort is in the presence of God. You will hear him say, 'My child, I know what it is like. It happened to me.' The prophet Hosea was bitterly let down by his wife Gomer.

She left him for a life of prostitution. God spoke to him and told him to go to the people of Israel with a message reinforced by his own circumstances. This was simply: what had happened to Hosea had happened to God in the sense that God's people had been as untrue to him as Hosea's wife had been to the prophet. Hosea probably never felt closer to God than at that stage. A divorced person may enter into deeper fellowship with God than could ever be imagined possible.

Secondly, remember, the believer's status as a child of God does not change when his or her marital status does. If you are a Christian, you are as close to God as any other believer, even though your marriage has ended. Jesus Christ is your justification. Nothing can alter that. When your marriage partner leaves, God is still your Father and you are still his child. He has not given up on you. His love for you is as strong as ever. Nothing in all creation is able to separate you from the love of God that is in Christ Jesus, your Lord. (See Romans 8:38–39.) Take heart from this fact.

Thirdly, make much of God's sovereignty. The Scripture teaches us clearly that even the wrath of man will praise him. (See Psalm 76:10.) The Bible's teaching about God's sovereignty is powerful, so much so that God even says, 'I form light and create darkness, I make well-being and create calamity, I am the LORD, who does all these things' (Isaiah 45:7). It has been said that if God could take the crucifixion and turn that into a blessing, he can do the same with a divorce. A child of God may even see the unfolding of God's purposes in the events in his life. Some of the best supporters of my ministry are divorced Christians. They are special for they have seen the hand of God even in what has happened to them, and they seem to understand so much more about trial and triumph.

Fourthly, do not let sin get the upper hand. It is to be expected that once love has curdled into hate after a once happily married couple have been torn apart, bitterness and resentment want to gain control. God's Word teaches, 'Beloved, never avenge yourselves, but leave it to the wrath of God, for it is written, "Vengeance is mine, I will repay, says the Lord." To the contrary, "if your enemy is hungry, feed him; if he is thirsty, give him something to drink; for by so doing you will heap burning coals on his head. Do not be overcome by evil, but overcome evil with good."' (Romans 12:19–21). In his parting message to his staff, former US President Richard Nixon said, 'Those who hate you do not win until you hate them back—and that will destroy you.' It does not pay to be vindictive. Jesus teaches his children to pray, 'And forgive us our debts, as we also have forgiven our debtors' (Matthew 6:12). Stephen forgave his murderers, and Jesus forgave those who crucified him. (See Acts 7:60; Luke 23:34.) In your agonizing experience, keep sin away from the door.

Fifthly, deal with depression the biblical way. Take those verses in Philippians 4:8–9 to heart. 'Whatever is true, whatever is honourable, whatever is just, whatever is pure, whatever is lovely, whatever is commendable, if there is any excellence, if there is anything worthy of praise, think about these things. What you have learned and received and heard and seen in me—practise these things, and the God of peace will be with you.'

Make it a practice every day to spend a few minutes in quiet meditation, considering all the blessings with which has God crowned your life. This will prevent you from becoming bitter. And it will do more than that. It will provide you with a positive and joyful disposition.

Sixthly, muster your energies to use your gifts in the local church. Romans 6 teaches that we should use our abilities for the Kingdom of God. Once the members of our body were used for sinful purposes, but now that we are Christians, we have to use them for the purpose of righteousness (see Romans 6:13). When a believer gets divorced, the Lord does not withdraw his gifts. He does not terminate the grace he gives his children to use their abilities when marriages dissolve because of unfortunate circumstances. (See Romans 11:29.) Go ahead and use them! A word of warning: you may need to expect that certain limitations and obstacles will be placed in the way. People may sometimes disqualify you from participating in Christian service because of your status. But remember, you are answerable to God alone. You may have failed in your marriage, but you are not a failure.

Seventhly, depend on God for strength in your tasks. One adult is missing from your home and you are alone. You became accustomed to sharing the load with someone else but now you are single. Keep in mind, Jesus was single too and he had to carry far greater responsibilities than you will ever have to. The Scripture says that as are your days, so shall your strength be (see Deuteronomy 33:25). God promised to be a never failing source of help to his people who need strength to perform his will.

Eighthly, believe God when he promises his special care. Divorce sometimes has serious economic consequences. Unfortunately, the innocent often have to bear the brunt of a marriage break up. One may become anxious and wonder how to make ends meet. God promises his children that they will never suffer serious want. Jesus said, 'Therefore, I tell you, do not be anxious about your life, what you will eat or what you will drink, nor about your body, what you will put on. Is not life more than food, and the body more than clothing? Look at the birds of the air: they neither sow nor reap nor gather into barns, and yet your heavenly Father feeds them. Are you not of more value than they?' (Matthew 6:25–26). Your standard of living may have to drop, but that is not the worst thing that can happen. Jesus said that life does not consist in the abundance of things a person possesses. (See Luke 12:15.) God will not fail you in providing for your daily necessities. Therefore, you may confidently trust him to care for you and yours in the days to come.

Ninthly, as a divorced person, be a testimony to your family and to the church. A Christian ought to excel even when circumstances are adverse. In that condition, he has the strongest possible testimony. Recently, a divorcee tearfully told me about her husband's incredible deceit and unfaithfulness. I was stunned. However, she continued to share her experience of God's grace at a time like that. She was, and is, a powerful testimony to what God can do for those who lean on him. Divorce is exceedingly painful, so much so that one divorced person expressed it as worse than death. Perfectly true, but even in the valley of the shadow of death, God comforts and even refreshes the soul of the believer who is united to Jesus by faith.

Lastly, have a Christian perspective of tragedy and triumph. Your marriage has ended, but not your hope. The Bible tells us 'that the sufferings of this present time are not worth comparing with the glory that is to be revealed to us' (Romans 8:18). The day is coming when the Lord will wipe every tear from his children's eyes. So great will be the glory of what we shall then have and experience, that all earthly sorrows will effectively be forgotten for ever.

Though you may have to carry a cross for a considerable period of time, not least of which is the pain of rejection and desertion, God is with you at present and the future is bright with hope for every child of Jesus. Look forward to coming glory and anticipate it with eagerness.

There is much to help you cope with the severance of your mariage ties. Take heart!

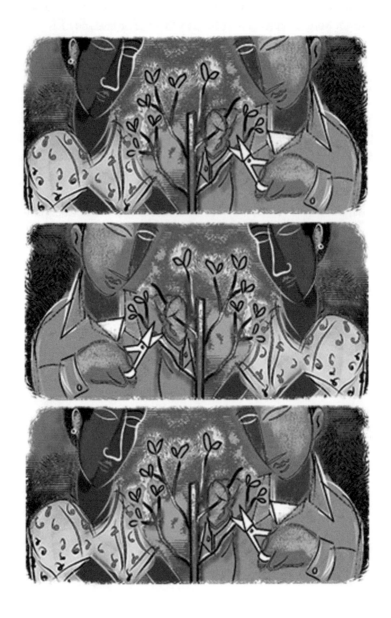

# Relationships of those divorced

The parting of the ways may have come for a previously married couple, but no man is an island, and they still have to live in a community with other people. They still have to maintain contact with those they were once close to and, whether they like it or not, because of either the children or for other reasons, they still have dealings with ex-partners, in-laws and other people, all affected by the event. How are they to handle these relationships?

To begin with, what about the ex-spouse? This is undoubtedly the most difficult of all. As a divorced person, you may feel you could never again say a kind word to him or her. Whenever you think of your 'has been', there is bitterness and anger in the heart. Research has proved that there is sometimes amazingly still love!

My advice is break with the past! It is over! You are no longer responsible for your ex-partner. Get rid of the vengeful spirit and under no circumstances try to get even with your former husband or wife. In talking about the person, never tell lies about him or her. Never call the person names. That only suggests emptiness on your part. When there is contact, as sometimes there has to be, do not do what others do when they fight over petty things. Do not be small-minded (for instance, do not leave the telephone to ring for an extra long time when you suspect that he or she is phoning, and when, eventually, you do pick it up, only immediately you put it down again). This is a less than mature, adult response. Never spy on your former spouse. Where does that get you? Never spread negative information among your mutual friends, whether true or false. What does that accomplish? Treat him or her with dignity and respect. That is how Jesus often treated his worst enemies. You have his example to guide you.

You need not necessarily break all ties with the in-laws. They often feel the pain of what has happened more than you realize. When you can, reassure them of your love and your esteem. They can often be a greater help than you possibly appreciate.

Unfortunately, in-laws are sometimes the cause of a divorce. When the Bible, for good reason, says that a man must leave his mother and father and cleave to his wife, the wisdom of God undoubtedly comprehended the tragic interference of parents in the lives of their married children. However, if this was not the case, you need to show ongoing love and friendship.

Your relationship with your children is crucially important. Even though you may have custody of these children, you still have to share them with your ex-spouse unless there are very strong and acceptable reasons for not doing so. Do not make it difficult for your former partner to have his share of them, as this will only cause resentment in the children sooner or later. Like it or not, they need both parents. Research has proved this time and again. Your hostility to the one you once loved must not be passed on to your offspring. They must be told at the time of the divorce that the relationship between each parent and the children remains intact even when the relationship between the parents has broken down.

Once a five-year-old boy told his mother that he wanted to cut himself in half so that he could be with both his parents at the same time. With immense feeling, he expressed that he did not like what had happened but would still maintain a relationship with both parents.

If you are a non-custodial parent, be trustworthy, punctual, understanding and sacrificial. It shatters a child when promises are broken, plans are jettisoned, and hopes are dashed.

If you remarry and have step-children, do not let them feel second-rate. If you have children of your own, this will be difficult but work at it so that they all feel that they get equal love and attention. Let the children know you care, you listen and have time for them. An expert on children of divorce has said, 'Most children do not really care about who did what to whom. What they care about is what is going to happen to them.'

Furthermore, help your children to keep the good memories of your past marriage alive. It is unwise to tear up old photo-albums because you can no longer stand the pictures which remind you of the past relationship. Your children need to keep those memories alive for themselves. As objectionable as they are to you, they are precious to the children.

Your relationship to the church must be stronger than ever before. The church has a responsibility to you, but you have a responsibility to the church as well. Do not expect the church members to give you extra special attention and do not become bitter towards believers who do not show the understanding you had hoped for. However, when God's children do show care and want to do things for you or invite you to their homes, do not be unduly suspicious of their motives. Only God sees the heart. It is not for you to attribute thoughts to others which may not even be true. As you mix with the people of God in the church, be circumspect in your relationships, especially with members of the opposite sex.

> **Your relationship to the church must be stronger than ever before. The church has a responsibility to you, but you have a responsibility to the church as well.**

Even though you are now single, be hospitable, for you still have a home and you still have a ministry.

Remember your relationship with other divorced persons. Do not become a group which is singled out. As there is an increasing number of you, and as you may resent married people talking about their home lives, aim to have a personal and wider ministry to those with whom you can identify. A common identity with sufferers of the same trial is a binding force.

Be very cautious of entering a new relationship with a possible new marriage partner. Be on your guard. I have had personal dealings with people who, in the interests of security, have rushed into a second marriage, only to regret it afterwards. Never be in a hurry. Ask others for their opinion and respect it. Sometimes your friends can see things better from the outside than you can, when love is temporarily blind.

If you consider remarriage, work out practical solutions to potential problems before the marriage and not afterwards. For example, think of the step-children, the allocation of finance, where to set up home. Resolve these before committing yourself.

Most important, remember your relationship with God. David still enjoyed deep communion with God after the tragic event where he was unfaithful to his vows. (See 2 Samuel 11.) Admittedly, he could only continue in fellowship with God after confessing his sin with a broken heart. (See Psalm 51 and 2 Samuel 12.) You will not enjoy the same sense of God's glory and presence if you self-righteously keep on blaming your ex-spouse for everything. Accept your part of the blame, confess it and get right with God. Glory in God who makes crooked paths straight and enjoy the Lord Jesus Christ as never before.

As a divorced person, your relationship with God is important as there is no other way in which you can hope to face the added difficulties of your new situation. I have often heard it said, 'If it had not been for God and the grace he gives, I could never have coped.' However, the grace of God is not necessarily automatically given. This grace is quite undeserved and unmerited, yet the Scriptures teach with equal emphasis that 'they who wait for the LORD shall renew their strength; they shall mount up with wings like eagles; they shall run and not be weary; they shall walk and not faint' (Isaiah 40:31).

The person who makes much of intense meditation in the Scriptures and on the glorious privilege of intercession with God is fortified for every need and every eventuality. Issues will crop up which will concern you and your relationship to your children. You may still have to discuss legal, technical and other matters with your ex-spouse which will require the wisdom of God and the control of the Holy Spirit. You cannot possibly expect to respond and behave in a God-honouring way if you do not walk with God as Enoch did. You need to resist temptation when you may be lured into another unwise, quick romance which could be more disastrous than anything known before. For you to be adequately prepared to stand up to this, you need to know the day-to-day experience of such fellowship with the Lord Jesus Christ that you will truly be kept by his great and wonderful power.

One divorced man I am acquainted with seems to know God best and enjoy him most in a close relationship. It appears that the agony of what happened to him only led to a fresh discovery of how glorious God really is, and Jesus Christ means so much to him now. This can be true of you, too. Of all the things you have to attend to, now that your marriage is a past event, make the most of knowing God and of knowing him well. It pays enormous dividends and you will, of all people, be most blessed.

## Sex after divorce

This very sensitive subject needs to be addressed for the sake of many.

An anonymous letter from a very kind, but concerned, person reached me in the mail. She cited the case of a couple who were divorced but remained friends. The reason for the divorce was a severe personality defect in the man, someone with an extremely low self-image and who made life nearly intolerable for his wife during their married years. There was violence and abuse and the marriage suffered one setback after another. The wife nearly caved in under the pressure. Now, after the divorce, they live separately and enjoy a much more tranquil relationship. They visit frequently, having eliminated the clashes which occurred while sharing bed and board, and yet they still satisfy their sexual needs from time to time.

What is wrong with that, seeing no third party was involved in the divorce? The ex-wife feels secure and protected from those unexpected outbursts of violence when the man lost control. He is able to have his needs fulfilled as and when it is necessary, without threatening his family as before.

The Bible clearly says, 'Trust in the Lord with all your heart, and do not lean on your own understanding' (Proverbs 3:5). It is very easy to pitch our understanding of things against the full and final teaching of the Word of God, especially when it seems a workable solution which does not have the sanction of God's Word. Before dealing with the case in point, allow me to make specific mention of some basic biblical principles.

According to the Bible, sex is only permissible within the marriage bond. 1 Corinthians 7:9 states that 'if they cannot exercise self-control, they should marry'. This is God's solution. There cannot be any doubt about that statement. Throughout the Scriptures, sex outside the marriage bond is summarily condemned. When Jacob's daughter, Dinah, had pre-marital sex with a man she proposed ultimately to marry, the matter was considered in a very serious light. Disaster followed, and the account can be found in Genesis 34.

The Bible considers divorce to be a full and final ending of a marriage relationship. It completely dissolves the marriage bond and, in the eyes of God, the couple concerned are no longer in the state of marriage union. Any physical union between the two is, therefore, fornication, until such time as they are reconciled. That reconciliation must be complete, that is, in a formal and proper marriage union. The very fact that 1 Corinthians 7:11 describes the divorced woman of a husband to whom she may still be reconciled as 'unmarried' implies that the status of a divorced couple is equal to that of a single person. Sex in that state is unlawful. The Lord most certainly does not consider a man and a woman to be husband and wife until such time as they restore their earlier marriage contract.

Now, we shall consider the case mentioned. Is there any compassion to be shown in that situation? Do we not pity both man and woman who, now being separate, have to some extent found each other? Not only do they now find life tolerable but they are also capable of continuing a friendship, even to the point of a close and physical union, without grief to anyone, within or without the family. It all seems to be such a perfect solution to a once intolerable problem. But, is it?

Can it enjoy God's blessing when it does not have the sanction of the Bible? Have all the problems of earlier tensions and conflicts been resolved? How is it that the present absence of a firm marriage contract and reduced contact between the two people can bring about such a change in the relationship? Is it not possible to address the previous issues which perhaps did not get sufficient attention at the time?

It seems a strong likelihood that the man found the full responsibility of being a husband and father so overwhelming that it got the better of him and, under that pressure, he was constantly breaking. With the weight of that off his shoulders, he is more relaxed and able to control himself better than before in the presence of his former wife. Surely, with biblical counselling, the same man would have been helped to cope far better as a husband and father, once his attitude to the relationship had improved. Outbursts of anger and violent reactions in the home are not merely the result of what is commonly called 'personality defects'. Often these occur either due to sin which had not been dealt with and is, therefore, unconfessed, or, as a result of stress which makes people feel they are simply not coping.

The man in this situation felt his responsibility so much that the threat of not fulfilling his calling as breadwinner or as head of the home had such a bearing on his thinking and emotions that he kept exploding. He needed to see he had no reason to feel threatened, particularly as a child of God, and he needed to experience the security of a deep relationship with Jesus Christ.

Another possibility is that his previous bad conduct may have been due to his taking advantage of his marital status and manipulating his wife and the domestic situation to his benefit. Now, as a divorced man, he recognizes that his wings have been clipped and he may enjoy a relationship with his former wife only on certain conditions. If this was the problem, he needs to confess his sin and be taught how, as a husband, he is there not only to rule but to serve at the same time, just as the Lord Jesus Christ, the King of the universe, lived as a servant of men and proved that life can be lived in a state of perpetual happiness as well as in perfect control of those circumstances that often seem to threaten one's mental balance.

Sex is a beautiful gift from God and may only be enjoyed within the marriage bond. The whole concept of a family living together, husband and wife, and children if any, is God's only ideal for happiness in the home on earth. There is absolutely no other blue-print for family life. There never will be. When problems arise, like the one cited, the real and actual causes for abnormal behaviour need to be discovered. Then these can be resolved properly with the help of the Holy

Spirit and under the leading of the Word of God.

When clashes occur in a marriage, it is not advisable to take the easiest escape route. Questions need to be asked. Why does he react in this way? When does he lose his temper? What factors contribute to it? How can they be dealt with?

Jesus is the Great Physician and he deals with our souls exactly as a good doctor deals with a person's body. His greatest challenge is dealing not so much with the symptoms as with the cause. The best doctors quickly and correctly diagnose the root cause of ills. Simply treating symptoms will never ever deal with the difficulty. The root of the matter is where we are. We must be careful not to use a term like 'personality perversion' without biblical support.

We need to look at ourselves in the light of God's Word and his truth. As our hearts are exposed to his judgement, we will discover precisely what gives rise to our temperaments and moods. When the Holy Spirit enables us to deal with these, we will find ourselves to be different people. May God help us all to live life in a healthy and orderly way.

# The church's ministry to the divorced person

In a day when we are surrounded by divorced people, the church has a splendid opportunity to exercise a ministry to hurting people. The Lord Jesus calls Christians 'the salt of the earth' and 'the light of the world' (Matthew 5:13–14). Without believers, the world would be a despicable mess. The world can be regarded almost as such, but it would be ten times worse were it not for alert, caring and compassionate disciples of Christ.

It is easy to condemn someone for being divorced. It is quite another thing to show sympathy, love and understanding. What an opportunity before us! How many divorced people have been brought into the Kingdom because Christians cared?

In the account of Jesus and the Samaritan woman in John 4, we find a woman who had been married and divorced several times, a woman who had become so disillusioned with the idea of marriage that she lived with a man to whom she was not married. Jesus did not condone this sin but he looked beyond that and saw a woman in need. He loved, cared and saved a soul.

What about the children of someone divorced? The Bible speaks about the fatherless and most assuredly refers to such children. God calls himself a Father to the fatherless. He is said to watch over the alien and to sustain the fatherless. (See Deuteronomy 10:18, 24:17; Psalm 68:5; 146:9; Jeremiah 22:3.)

Remember, the divorced person is one who suffers and yearns for encouragement and comfort. What form does this suffering take? There is a poor self-image. It is often the result of long-term criticism because the ex-partner used to be disparaging, belittling, insulting and judgemental, to the point that the poor victim believed some of the things said. The psychological damage can be intense and it takes a long time to heal.

This is precisely where the church has a vital ministry. Jesus gives people with low self-esteem a sense of worth when he calls them to repentance and faith and when he makes them his children.

Then there is the loss of income which often leads to a drop in social status. Pride is easily wounded, especially if such a person once lived in a reasonably well-to-do community. Now he finds himself in a completely different setting because of the economical impact of the divorce. This is where the church should make the person feel loved and accepted. Quality of life has nothing to do with quantity of possessions. Some of the happiest and most fulfilled people possess very little of this world's goods. Often it is God's purpose to bring us to a position where we have to learn to live with less so that we may appreciate all the more the tremendous richness of God's fellowship in Christ. Learning to cope on a lower income can be an exciting challenge and some of the purposes of God may be discovered in the changes in lifestyle.

The divorced person also experiences a tremendous emotional drain. Tears have flowed for months on end. Frustrations, anxieties, fears within and fears without, and deep disappointments have taken their toll. The person has undergone a severe beating because of the stress and strain experienced in the tearing apart of two people. There is a ministry to people like these.

A further factor to be considered can be summed up in the word 'overburdened'. One victim of a broken marriage described her experience in the following way: 'In a marriage the responsibilities of the day are carried by two people. Now virtually the same load is borne by one person.' This is particularly true if there are children. The sheer weight of having to carry the ordinary burdens, as well as the responsibilities of an adult with a family, can be extremely demanding. This calls for sensitivity and practical help from the people of God.

Then there is the very real experience of loneliness. The reason why God ordained marriage in the first place was to solve the problem of loneliness. An ideal marriage does just that. Having tasted the richness of companionship, the divorced person does not only feel alone, but thoroughly deprived. There is no one in the home to discuss those peculiar concerns which are everybody's cares; no one to consult about decisions to be made; no one to ease the yoke of trials common to man. Loneliness can be one of the most painful experiences in life.

In addition, such a person also begins to taste exhaustion on a scale never known before. This is particularly true of a woman who has to find work to make ends meet and, having done justice to a full day's work, still has to face the prospect of coming home to all the usual household chores. She has no time for herself and very little for her children. Is this not where believers should be quick to come to the fore with whatever help can be offered?

And, finally, after all the experiences mentioned, depression sets in. Small wonder, as such an accumulation of discomforts can only lead to a state of distress, unless there are caring people to take note and to fulfil what the Scriptures call the law of Christ, which is bearing one another's burdens. (See Galatians 6:2.)

**The church is meant to make the divorced person feel as much at home in the fellowship as any other believer.**

It is important to remember not to mention the marital status of the person divorced when he or she is being referred to. This will be like rubbing salt into the already painful wound. Divorce is not an unforgivable sin. A child of God whose marriage has ended is as much a child of God as any other believer. God's love to a divorced Christian is no less than to any of his other children. The church is meant to make the divorced person feel as much at home in the fellowship as any other believer and it is the duty of Christians to ensure that the stigma attached to divorce is felt the least here. Such a person should not be perceived so much as being divorced, but rather as being a brother or sister in Christ.

If Christians glory in the fact that God cleans the slate of our past sins and failures, and that he glories in giving us a fresh start in life, we must be consistent. No one in the family of God should feel either unwanted or awkward.

All who are redeemed by the blood of Christ need to know that they have a vital place in the body of Christ. The divorced person needs us as much as we need him or her and we cannot do without the prayer support, the moral encouragement and the gifts which come from that important quarter.

In view of the fact that divorce will be an ongoing phenomenon in the world and even in the church, it is essential that the church remembers to stand by the unhappy victim of divorce proceedings when these are underway. Very little is as traumatic and painful as having to go through the court process leading to the ultimate severance of marital ties. The painfulness of it all, the lack of sleep because of the stress and the uncertainty regarding the future is something very few people can handle on their own. The people of God ought to be quick to come to the assistance of the one who is suffering in these situations. It is every bit our responsibility to help with the children, if there are any, as with the person suffering most. We should be available when we are needed and thus prove ourselves to be Christian friends.

Lastly, be mindful of the church's special ministry to the children of a broken home. These children feel insecure as they wonder, 'If my parents rejected each other, will they not do the same to me?' They need reassurance of love and attention, and we should not despise their seeming clamour to be noticed. This continues when remarriage occurs, as they wonder then, 'Will the new step-parent take the attention I need?'

The children of God have a responsibility to divorced people and their children. This is a wonderful ministry to offer. Christians are not to leave people to carry their burdens on their own. That is not what Jesus did. He spent his entire life on earth serving others. He said he came not to be ministered to, but to minister and to give his life a ransom for many. (See Matthew 20:28 and Mark 10:45.) We cannot call ourselves his followers if we do not do the same. Rise to the occasion. Be on the lookout for those who have suffered the agony of divorce and help them in their time of need.

# The children of a divorce

This is one of the most important aspects of this curse of modern society—the children of those whose marriages flounder. The children are the victims.

There are several things one ought to know with respect to children from a broken marriage. First, and most important, it is vital to strive for the child's conversion to Christ. Often it is said that knowing Jesus as personal Saviour from sin, in the heart-breaking situation where parents have parted, has been an enormous help in the trauma. To have a meaningful personal relationship with Jesus when other relationships are breaking is a lifesaver.

An early conversion is a wonderful gift from God for it ensures an ability to handle crises which nothing else can equal. Do everything you can to help your child into the Kingdom of God. Dr Horatius Bonar said, concerning the spiritual history of 253 converts with whom he was familiar, 'Saved under 20 years of age-, 138; between 20 and 30 years—85; between 30 and 40 years—22; between 40 and 50 years—4; between 50 and 60 years—3; between 60 and 70 years—1. Over 70—not one!' You see how important it is to lead your child to Christ.

While divorce can devastate a child's life, grace always makes a difference! Little five year-old William stood barefoot and cold in a street in Glasgow and wondered why no one gave him food when he had had nothing to eat for a day and a half. At six and a half, he went to work in a factory putting the heads on pins for twelve hours a day, earning a shilling a week. What chance in life had this poor, starved little creature? When he was seventeen, he heard the gospel for the first time, believed it and received the Saviour. He has been in heaven for many years now, but a monument to his work on earth remains. The orphan homes of Scotland were the result of his thinking and initiative.

Mary Slessor went to work in a factory when she was eleven to help supply the needs of her younger brothers and sisters because her father was a drunkard.

She was neither tall nor strong and, of course, not well educated. How could such a sorrowful and thwarted childhood lead to a useful and blessed womanhood? Someone warned her to escape the fire that will never be extinguished. She listened and came to the children's Saviour. Mary Slessor grew to be a household name in Christian circles for she brought incalculable spiritual and material help to a part of West Africa.

God's purposes for children raised in adverse circumstances do not change. Help those from a broken marriage to see that!

Several things need to be kept in mind when you go through a divorce. Whether you like it or not, children are deeply, deeply affected. Many of them, in fact most of them, hide their real feelings. In order to lessen the damage done to them, and to make some good come for them from this trial, consider the following:

When parents decide to get divorced, tell the children together. As hard as this might be, put your pride aside, and break the news in a responsible and mature way. It is vital for the child's own self-assurance that both mother and father act together. This prevents misinformation, as a child can easily draw conclusions from what appears to be varying interpretations of the cause if he or she is told separately.

The child needs to be reassured of the continuing bond between him or her and both parents. The child needs to understand that while the earlier love and attachment between the parents has broken down, the same does not apply to the relationship of parents to child. Each parent must stress his or her ongoing love and affection for all the children.

Children need both their parents. In the heat of a marriage break up, judgement is easily impaired. Parents fighting for the custody of the child often make out that the little ones, or older if that, do not need the other partner. Research has shown that even where there has been neglect or abuse from one of the parents, there is still a deep inner longing for a relationship with both. It is highly selfish and proud of parties who are parting to overlook the deep spiritual and mental needs of the children. Children must feel loved and wanted. However much the dissolution of the marriage affects the husband and the wife, it is absolutely essential for the children to receive adequate love and affection.

If this does not happen, they will get it where you do not want them to seek it, which can be disastrous. They need time with both parents.

Do not expect a child to take the place of a missing parent. I have seen the distressing situation where ill-advised onlookers will tell a young boy, who faces the prospect of a life without his father, that he now has the responsibility to take his dad's place. That is wrong. The custodial parent must never deny the children time with the non-custodial parent.

Furthermore, these children need understanding. They may begin to show signs of withdrawal. It is cruel to tell such a one to pull himself together when there are deep hurts and insecurities to be understood and addressed.

When parents part ways, discipline must be consistent. It is no use making up with expensive gifts. If anything, this is highly inadvisable. The same standards of conduct which prevailed before must continue and the same consequences for bad behaviour must be meted out.

Allow them to spend time with their grandparents. If those associations had value in the past, they will have worth in the future. To cut children off from those dear folk will be to their permanent detriment. Grandparents, by virtue of their maturity and experience, have a positive contribution to make.

Tell the children about God's special care for single-parent children. The Scriptures repeatedly refer to God as one who cares for the fatherless and so speaks of the concern of an omniscient God who knows and understands the fears and anxieties of children who have witnessed trouble in the home between their parents. The very best a mother or father can do is to direct the thoughts of the children to the one who stands above all and who can do more than anyone else.

God is also the only one who can repair the damage done by the sin which has shattered the vows which once were meant to keep a home together.

Discuss the divorce with them. They are not fools and to suppress conversation about something so real to them is to deny them the opportunity of being open and frank about an unforgettable event in their lives.

As I have shown, suffering is acute for children as they witness the cleavage of their parents in divorce and the disintegration of the world as they have known it in their tenderest years. How can we mitigate this? It is so very important. The gospel is absolutely unique in pouring the balm of Gilead into hurting wounds. The Bible deals with suffering uniquely. Human philosophies are all empty and destitute of the authority of our Triune God. The Bible alone reveals a Saviour as the great physician who heals. The Scriptures teach us something about suffering which no human moralizing can. They teach us that God appoints suffering for us all and it draws us closer to him and his love when we pass through the fires of affliction. (See Isaiah 43:1–3; Romans 5:3–5 and 2 Timothy 2:3.). Also, uniquely, it sets our sufferings in the framework and light of eternity and teaches us to appreciate the perfection of the state which will be ushered in when Jesus Christ returns in glory.

Be trustworthy with your children. Their faith has been shattered, at least their faith in their parents. Restore their ability to trust by being punctual when you make appointments with them, by keeping your promises to them, and by maintaining your responsibility as parents to them. Any further erosion of their confidence in you is simply not fair.

Be mature enough to teach them from your mistakes which pitfalls to avoid in order to ensure a happy marriage of their own one day. Under no circumstances should you leave them with the impression that, since your marriage did not work, the prospect of theirs failing is equally high. God ordained marriage in the first place and he meant it to be happy and holy. Even though yours has failed, there are countless others which have not. Cherish happiness in the marriage bond for each of your children.

When you are under stress because of your state, do not treat your children as fools. Let them hear you pray about your problems. Discuss with them your future plans and draw them into these. They want to be part of whatever lies ahead and it can cheer their spirits when they see you deliberately acknowledging them in your goals for your common future.

Now that you are a single parent, deal with them at their level and do not have unrealistic expectations of them because of your needs. If you want to strengthen the bond with your children, read the Scriptures and pray with them.

Remember, your inability to keep your marriage together does not mean that you are a poor parent. While there are inseparable connections between marriage and parenting, many people, whose marriages have broken up, are still capable of excelling as fathers and mothers. This is your opportunity to do just that. Your children will be grateful for your ongoing sacrifices which, in turn, will ensure a happier life for them.

# The scars of divorce

Sometimes one discovers a piece of literature so good that it should be shared. A tract which I found needs to be read by all. It is the account of a girl who anonymously called herself 'A Wounded Heart'. Maybe this little tract will stem the tide of an ever-increasing number of divorces, as divorce is a very selfish affair. It does not consider the children. Perhaps it tries to compensate for their loss in monetary terms by a generous provision for their maintenance. But it can never undo the psychological damage to the heart of a son or a daughter who has to work through this just like anyone else affected.

It is perfectly true that God can heal the heart as none other can. On the other hand, we must not think that we can get away with sin all that easily. We need far more empathy than we have, especially considering that Jesus solemnly warned that if we put a stumbling block before children, some of whom he received and blessed so heartily, we are in danger of severe judgement.

The tract reads:

'Please, please don't sign them! O Daddy, don't sign those papers!' My pleadings must have added greatly to my father's burden, but the pen held firmly in his hand continued to write his name on the final paper.

Thus was my world destroyed and I with it, for on that day something died in the heart of a child. A child? In years, yes, but the child pleading in the divorce court that day would never again be a carefree little girl. For now my mommy and daddy were divorced. It was a big word and a hateful one. What it meant to grown-ups I did not know, but what it meant to me is a story that can never be told. Right now it meant that the home we had known existed no longer. To us children our home was our world, with both Mother and Daddy essential parts of it. But that world had suddenly crumbled. Like a storm that strikes suddenly and leaves you to pick up the pieces, so life had suddenly turned our home inside out and upside down. Much of the shock lay in the fact that the ones destroying it were the two who had been our very security and life. From now on the family must be divided. I was told to choose between my mother and father—I could not have both, though I loved both and wanted them, both of them, to love me. Each was so necessary to me; how could I turn my back on one and say I wanted the other more?

I remembered nights when I was sick and how my mother kept vigil— how she had fed me and tended to my needs. Surely, she loved me! When things troubled me I had always gone to her and her explanations had banished childish fears. I had great faith in my mother. Nor could I doubt my father's love or the close place I had in his heart. Often my brothers had sent me to dad when they wanted some favour, knowing he seldom refused me. This special place I had with daddy was perhaps because I was so like him and we understood each other so well. I had deep respect for my father—but how could I compare it with what I felt for mother? And how could I make a decision that would separate me from either?

This was the down payment in the price of divorce—and the children had to pay. To parents who are still counting the cost, I plead the cause of your children! If you subject them to the agony of choosing between the parents they love, something wonderful has to die in their hearts during the unnatural struggle that choice entails.

Years have passed, but I still shudder at the memory of the day I left our home—with my mother. Daddy cried like a child and then just stood and stared into space. I have wondered what went through his mind then. He had worked so hard to do right by his family, and now all he had built was gone. Was part of his grief due to the fact that missing from the circle of his motherless children was his only daughter? Was he thinking of what might have been? In my mind there is no doubt of what might have been: theirs could have been a successful marriage had they determined to keep the home intact— had both, or even one, been willing to sacrifice personal feelings. As far back as my memory goes, I remember my parents quarrelling. Like all quarrels, these were born of selfishness and stubbornness, with neither willing to give in to the other. Foolish advice was, 'Separate if you can't get along; it will be better for the children' (Better to crush six young hearts than for one or two to bear small hurts? Better the blow should fall on six lives, young and tender, not old enough to know why they must be separated from one another?)

Bitter protests and tears were vain, for divorce courts do not consider human hearts when they collect their dues. Mother and Daddy were to be 'free', but we children were not. I became a slave to despair. The quarrels? They ceased, to be sure, but cries of heartbroken children took their place, and I, for one, longed to hear those quarrels if only it meant I could have my mother and daddy back!

This story is my own—the plea I make is that of my own heart, though my brothers too could write their stories and neighbours in our small town could add to it. Perhaps it is just a familiar story—daddy, too busy to do the little things that count so much and having to neglect his six and eight year-old boys. My little brother longed for his mother, but his loss and grief gave expression to meanness; so he became a problem child in school. My teenage brothers became involved with the law to the extent that they spent a night in jail. I realized even then that this, too, was part of the price of divorce—that the children pay.

Perhaps a girl needs her mother even more than do the boys. I seemed to be cut the deepest and to suffer the most. The shock of that day in court was indelibly printed on my memory, but I had only begun to taste the bitter portion dealt to a child of divorced parents. With daddy thrust out of my life, my brothers gone, my heart fastened more tenaciously than ever on mother, and words cannot express the shock that was mine when I found her in the arms of another man. In that instant I knew utter desolation. I had lost my father—now my mother no longer belonged to me! Another man—a stranger to me—had taken her and this discovery completely changed and embittered my life. Emotions that had been sealed within me now broke forth in endless weeping. Bitterness enveloped me like a cloud and resentment made it impossible for me to speak peaceably to mother. On the back of confused emotions came the resolve that no one else should have her—she belonged to me and daddy! I became crazed with the idea that I must win her from the one who I felt was the cause of my sorrow. A showdown had to come. One day I found mother and her boyfriend with other friends in the front yard. Blind despair and a lingering hope gripped me, and for me that gathering became a court session, with a child as prosecuting attorney and the neighbours as jurors. The desperation that filled my heart poured out: our need of daddy, our need of the home we had left—'Oh, please mommy, let us go back and be happy!'

Artists may paint human suffering but neither artist's brush nor writer's pen can recapture the horror of the moment when a child realizes it has lost the battle for its mother's love. One day she had been my mother—the next, she was a stranger whose only feeling seemed to be displeasure at the scene her unreasonable child was causing. Neighbours pitied and tried to comfort, but their words did not reach me—I knew only departed hope. I had failed, and no failure had ever involved so much. I may have been in a state of shock as I found my way back to the old home. A few weeks before I had been in this home—a happy, confident child, but as I entered the familiar yard there was no joy in my heart—no anticipation or eagerness. Daddy met me at the door and seemed thankful I had returned, but he found to his sorrow that it was not the same little girl who had come back. Shock and grief caused youth to flee, and with it had gone laughter and joy.

He tried but he was not able to save me from the depths of despair to which I sank. I wept until tears no longer came. Many pitied but there was no healing for my wounded heart. When we heard that mother had re-married, great bitterness possessed me. Grief had so eaten away at my life that I became hard and rebellious. The faith that my mother had destroyed caused me to lose confidence in everyone, even my father, and I felt that everyone was against me. Nothing mattered anymore. When daddy corrected me, I thought that he too had turned against me, and I rebelled under his authority.

I left him and stayed with anyone who would have me. Later, harsh circumstances compelled me to go back to my mother and her husband. I must have been a shadow of the past to them, and I lived with the stinging reality that I was not wanted. Yet every fibre of my being craved to be loved. Violent arguments—a war of hate—began between me and the intruder. Strain began to show on mother's face and, in my misery, I found secret consolation in the fact. My strained emotions became a physical illness, for the human system can be overtaxed just so long before something breaks. Clouds of gloom settled over me; nightmares caused me to run screaming through the house. I suffered cruelly and being alone most of the time actually developed a fear of people. I succumbed completely to shattered nerves.

I wish I could take the hand of every parent harbouring the thought of divorce and lead you back with me into the valley through which I have come. If the hurt of an innocent child's heart, the bitter shock of a tender life, the tears of the unwanted, misplaced child, the horror and gloom could be called to witness in the divorce courts, no child would again have to walk the dreadful road that starts with the signing of those final papers in the divorce courts. Instead, the tears would become your own and in the valley you would realize that the ones who suffer in divorce and re-marriage are the innocent children.

Thank God, in my struggles through the darkness I met the Saviour and slowly—very slowly—began to live again. Since that time I have married and, at one time, it seemed that I would fail as my parents had. But through sacrifices and love, I was able to prove that marriage can be made to last. My wonderful husband and lovely children are my reward after having, as Job, drunk scourging like water. Many will say, 'But my case is different.' I contend that every marriage can be made to last if either husband or wife will fight to that end. Mine did not succeed overnight, but every effort proved worthwhile for, through sacrifices of my own feelings, I brought out qualities in my husband that I had not known existed. God alone knows the joys I now reap from every battle I fought—with myself—instead of with my husband. I had to learn to give when I would rather take, to smile when my heart rebelled, and to hold

my peace and let God speak for me. But it was worth all it cost when compared to the reward—one of the most happy marriages in the world.

From experience, I know divorce is not the answer—sacrifice is. You who contemplate divorce—I beg of you, remember me. Hold that child of yours in your arms more closely and, in pity, spare him that which I have had to endure and can never forget.'

I hope this testimony spoke to your heart as it did to mine. It warns us to be on our guard against the faintest manifestation of selfishness in our own hearts. It tells us to consider others before ourselves. It warns us not to trifle with holy ordinances such as the divine institution of marriage which God intends us to keep. How I would love to see every home a happy home! God can do what we cannot.

# Postscript: Together for ever

For all the hurt and heartache of divorce, there is something every divorcee can look forward to, provided Christ is loved and known. Believers are married to Christ by faith and are in a bond higher and holier than any bond on earth. In Romans 7:2–4, believers are said to be married to him who is raised from the dead. The apostle Paul told the believers in Corinth that he had betrothed them to one husband, and that husband was Christ. (See 2 Corinthians 11:2.) When the principles of a healthy marriage are spelt out in Ephesians 5:22–33, the apostle summed it all up by saying, 'This mystery is profound, and I am saying that it refers to Christ and the church' (v. 32). Addressing his people in the Old Testament, God wanted them to know that 'your Maker is your Husband' (Isaiah 54:5). When the saints finally reach their glorious destination, they will be 'as a bride adorned for her husband' (Revelation 21:2). The bond will never be severed. There will never be the saying 'until death us do part' for 'He will wipe away every tear from their eyes, and death shall be no more, neither shall there be mourning nor crying nor pain any more, for the former things have passed away' (Revelation 21:4). Among those who will experience this eternal bliss, will be thousands who had once experienced the painfulness of a divorce when they had lived on earth. Their being bonded to the greatest Lover ever to unite himself to those for whom he bled and died will be for ever and ever. Divorce will never be thought of again when all who have known his saving power will experience the exhilaration expressed in the Song of Solomon 2:3–4: 'With great delight I sat in his shadow, and his fruit was sweet to my taste, he brought me to the banqueting house, and his banner over me was love.'

## God's prescription for a healthy marriage

ANDREW OLIVER

ISBN 978 1 84625 095 8

PAPERBACK 160PP

God's prescription
For a healthy marriage and family

Andrew Oliver

The family is under threat. Contemporary culture and changes in legislation are seeking to redefine its structure, parents are increasingly giving over to the state the responsibility of disciplining their children, and homes are constantly bombarded by immoral images of the 'family' through TV. The great need today is to return to biblical principles for family life. The Bible is God's manual for the people he created in his image, and therefore it has much to say on this crucial issue. Here, Andy Oliver guides us helpfully through the biblical teaching on marriage and family life, and emphasizes the need to follow God's Word if we are to build solid foundations for a healthy family.

'Across Europe, and, indeed, the Western world, the crisis in marriage and family life is impacting Christian and non-Christian alike, and Andy Oliver's book provides a timely reminder of God's good purposes for us. His approach is thought-provoking and uncompromising and, while you might not agree with every application, you will benefit greatly from this refreshingly direct and practical introduction to what the Bible teaches.'

—*Jonathan Lamb, Author, Director of Langham Preaching (Langham Partnership International) and former Associate General Secretary of IFES*

Andy Oliver comes from Northern Ireland, where he ran his own small business before entering full-time Christian ministry. He studied theology at the Irish Baptist College (then situated in Belfast), and has a BD and MTh from Queens University

Belfast and a PGCE from Cambridge University. Since 1999 Andy has been engaged in missionary service and pastoral ministry in Albania, and he is a frequent speaker at university student meetings on behalf of BSKSH (IFES Albania). He and his wife, Ela, have two daughters, Rakela and Emma, and a son, Jack.

- **A strongly applicatory book which looks practically and biblically at marriage and the family**
- **Considers matters such as headship, submission and the preparation of the family for eternity**
- **Includes detailed study and discussion questions**

## Courting Disaster— Should Christians and non-Christians date each other?

NEIL RICHARDSON

ISBN 978 1 84625 007 1

PAPERBACK 80PP

There is one purpose in life: 'to glorify God, and to enjoy him for ever'. This book aims to encourage us to please God by submitting our wills to his in our romantic relationships. Neil Richardson explains that the teaching of the Bible is that Christians should not go out with non-Christians, and he thoroughly explores the various issues involved. He looks at points such as:

- Why it is wrong to go out with a non-Christian;
- Some of our motives for wanting these relationships;
- What the eternal consequences are if we disobey the Bible's teaching;
- Our objections to obeying this teaching.

In addition, he offers some helpful advice to parents of children who might be involved in relationships with unbelievers, and deals with some ethnic issues which might arise.

'This little book hits the nail on the head! If we are going to call ourselves Christians, then we should submit to the authority of God's holy Word, the Bible... As Neil Richardson has elegantly and biblically defended, the Bible, not our emotions and feelings, must be our guide in these most important areas of life. I recommend this book for singles and parents alike!'

—*Dr Jobe Martin, DMD, Th.M,* founder of Biblical Discipleship Ministries, author of The Evolution of a Creationist and What God says about relationships, marriage and family

'This book is a thoughtful, practical and—above all—passionate plea for

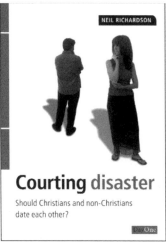

## Courting disaster
Should Christians and non-Christians date each other?

wholehearted discipleship in an area of great relevance for all Christian young people and youth group leaders'.

—*Christopher Ash,* Director of the Cornhill Training Course and author of Marriage: Sex in the service of God

Neil Richardson was born in Turkey to 'tentmaker' missionary parents. He was raised in west London and came to repentance and faith at the age of thirteen. He read English at University College, London, (where he led the Christian Union) and took his Post Graduate Certificate of Education at King's, London. After teaching for five years and then studying at Cornhill Training Course, he is now assistant pastor at Derby Road Baptist Church, Watford, England. His interests include open air evangelism, old people, kids, good books, music, clean comedy, games and running as far as he can.

- **Addresses a common issue**
- **Realistic approach to the situation**
- **Written in an engaging way**
- **Includes photocopyable synopsis to summarize key points for use in youth meetings, etc**

BRIAN AND BARBARA EDWARDS

No longer **Two**

A Christian guide for engagement and marriage

'Brian and Barbara Edwards have put us in their debt, providing us with this excellent treatment of such a vital topic'
Evangelical Times

Day One

### No Longer Two
A Christian guide for engagement and marriage

BRIAN AND BARBARA EDWARDS

LARGE FORMAT PAPERBACK

144 PAGES

978 1 903087 00 8

With more than one in three marriages ending in divorce, the institution is more under threat than ever and divorce among Christians is at an all time high. In response to this, churches now offer pre-marital counselling for engaged couples. Some clergy now refuse to marry a couple unless they have taken such a course. 'No Longer Two' is a highly acclaimed marriage preparation guide offering an exciting way of working together to build a strong marriage based upon the clear teaching and common sense of the Bible. Whether or not you are familiar with the Bible, you will find this an easy-to-use guide—perfect for individuals and groups alike.

REFERENCE: NL2

**Quite simply one of the best books on the market today on the subject of marriage**
THE MONTHLY RECORD

'Brian and Barbara Edwards have put us in their debt, providing us with this excellent treatment of such a vital topic'
EVANGELICAL TIMES

# What's so special about No Longer Two?

**Thorough treatment:** chapter by chapter the subject is dealt with from the Bible with practical application

**Bible studies** ensure that the reader actually has to get involved—perfect for individuals, great for groups.

# About Day One:

## Day One's threefold commitment:

- To be faithful to the Bible, God's inerrant, infallible Word;
- To be relevant to our modern generation;
- To be excellent in our publication standards.

I continue to be thankful for the publications of Day One. They are biblical; they have sound theology; and they are relative to the issues at hand. The material is condensed and manageable while, at the same time, being complete—a challenging balance to find. We are happy in our ministry to make use of these excellent publications.

*JOHN MACARTHUR, PASTOR-TEACHER, GRACE COMMUNITY CHURCH, CALIFORNIA*

It a great encouragement to see Day One making such excellent progress. Their publications are always biblical, accessible and attractively produced, with no compromise on quality. Long may their progress continue and increase!

*JOHN BLANCHARD, AUTHOR, EVANGELIST AND APOLOGIST*

Visit our website for more information and to request a free catalogue of our books.

www.dayone.co.uk